THE CHRISTIAN *vs.* THE UNIVERSITY

Fighting the Battle of Ideas
On the College Campus

THE CHRISTIAN

— vs. —

THE UNIVERSITY

Fighting the Battle of Ideas
On the College Campus

GARRISON McKEEN CATTELL

ISBN: 978-1-105-55234-2

CONTENTS

THE BATTLE THAT LIES AHEAD

D ear Aaron,

I would be honored to correspond with you during your first semester in college. After all, I am your favorite uncle. Oh, and no need to remind me that I am your only uncle! You are the first of the nieces and nephews to go to college, so I hope to learn a lot from your experience. As you know, your Dad and I did not become Christians until later in life, so I do not know what it is like to grow up in the Church and then go out into the world. I would also like to say that I understand your concern about your parents, but I am sure they will come around. They'll eventually get serious about their Christianity. Maybe you can be an example to them.

I see from your e-mail that it hasn't taken you long to realize that your Christianity will be sorely tested in your new environment. In my years of evangelizing at Penn State, I have seen many young freshmen lose their religion. I must admit though that most of them seemed pretty poorly trained when they arrived. I don't know what churches are doing these days, but it seems as if most of them are not doing an adequate job training their young people. As a result, they are sending them off to college like sheep to the slaughter.

Don't get me wrong, I certainly believe that the religious and moral agenda that dominates at colleges and universities these days can be defeated, but only if the churches wake up and realize that we are in a war for our kids' souls, and stop sending them off to battle virtually defenseless. Of course, I am not letting parents off the hook. We oftentimes get so caught up in the daily activities of life, that we forget to do the one thing that is most important, and that is to make sure our kids are Christian in more than name only. As for your question as to why there seems to be an anti-Christian agenda at many universities today, I will certainly give you my opinion, but first a quick history lesson is in order.

Modern day liberalism, which is the disease you will be fighting over the next four years, had its beginnings in the European Enlightenment. This was a decidedly anti-Christian movement with atheistic leanings. It came to the U.S. with the founding fathers, but really gathered momentum in the late 1800s under the guise of humanism and burst onto the college and university scene in the late 1960s. Staying true to its Enlightenment origins, the liberalism of the '60s seeks to draw America away from her Christian roots, to what amounts to an atheistic worldview. This is not to say that every liberal is an atheist, but generally liberals do not want us, as a society, to look to God for our understanding of the world.

On the other hand, I think most people would agree that America began as a Protestant nation. By this I do not mean we were a theocracy but that the vast majority of us believed in Protestant Christianity, and we ordered our society accordingly. As far as putting this religion into practice there were, of course, low times and high times, with the low times punctuated by periods of revival. One such revival took place during World War II, as many thought the signs of the times were pointing towards the end of the world. The war eventually ran its course with no end of the world in sight. So the men came home to do what men always do after being away for an extended period of time. That's right; they made babies! The result of all this activity was what we call the baby boomer generation, which came of age in the '60s and '70s. Unfortunately the revival during the war didn't last long, nor did it have much depth, and by the time the boomers reached college, the Christianity of their parents was more cultural than vital.

As parents, the World War II generation, following the advice of Dr. Benjamin Spock (amongst others), tended to pamper their kids, not wanting them to go through what they had faced during the Great Depression and the War. For reasons unknown to me, it didn't occur to them that it was going through these experiences that gave them the strong character that we still admire today.

As a result of this pampered upbringing and the largely atheistic worldview they were learning at the universities, the philosophy of life for the boomers was to obtain as much pleasure as one could with as little responsibility as possible. All of this, combined with the possibility of being drafted into an unpopular war, compelled this new generation to begin challenging the way of life that was handed down to them. Of course, Christianity, with its asceticism and emphasis on self-control, was at the root of this way of life, and unfortunately the baby boomers' elders were unprepared to defend it.

This is why I do not believe that what happened in the '60s was merely a sexual revolution; rather, more so it was a religious one. Christianity was overthrown, and a sort of liberal secularism was put in its place. This form of liberalism is not necessarily devoid of spirituality, but it is dead set against traditional Christianity.

If we look at the movements that came out of the '60s and are still on campus today, we can see that the one thing they have in common is that they are anti-Christian. Whether it is the pro-abortion movement, the homosexual agenda, radical feminism and environmentalism, the drug culture, sexual promiscuity, easy divorce, etc., it is all anti-Christian. This is what they have in common, this is what binds them together, and this is what you will be dealing with on campus over the next four to five years.

I hope this gives you a little background on what you will be facing in the years to come. I believe that when our faith is challenged it can become stronger, or it can die, depending on how we respond. So if I may give you some advice, don't take what your professors say at face value. I realize they can be intimidating, but if they teach anything that goes against your faith, search out the Christian response. I guarantee you that after two thousand years we have heard it all, and we have a reasonable answer to every objection. Please continue to write. I may not have all the answers, but I'll do what I can to help.

Love,
Uncle Greg

THE CULTURE WAR

Dear Aaron,

Yes, I guess you can label what is going on as a culture war. Certainly it is termed that way quite often. Remember, that even though our present society was set up by modern day liberals, it really isn't a war of conservative vs. liberal, or even traditionalist vs. secularist, but that of Christian vs. anti-Christian. If the anti-Christian forces are successful in removing Christian standards from society, the results could be disastrous. Therefore every Christian should in some way be engaged in the battle.

As I mentioned last time, we as Americans used to see life through some form of Protestant Christian eyes. We were never an officially Christian country, but we chose our morals, and saw ourselves and the world around us from that perspective. We certainly made many mistakes and were not always true to our beliefs, but we had an objective standard by which we could be judged and corrected. In other words, our Christianity gave us boundaries that said we could go this far and no further. If we transgressed those boundaries, we could be chastised and brought back.

When we threw off Christianity in the late '60s and early '70s, we replaced it with a Godless standard that relied upon human reason and the will of the majority. This is a subjective standard, which by its very nature has no inherent boundaries. In addition, there is no way to judge whatever arises from it as being right or wrong. In other words, whatever the majority declares becomes what is right, and the only way to change it is by some future majority. Unfortunately, there is no way to judge either one, because there is no absolute standard by which to judge.

We can see an example of this in the present-day debate over homosexual marriage. Marriage between one man and one woman is one of the last vestiges of a Christian worldview left in our society. Since the family is the foundation of society, if we were to do away with the Christian understanding of marriage, we would change the very foundation of our culture. Our worldview would no longer be based on Christianity but on secularism. As a result, there would no longer be an absolute standard by which we could make moral judgments on anything—much less, who should and should not be getting married.

If we do not look to God for our moral understandings, why is anything inherently wrong? Is it written in the stars that murder and rape are wrong? Does the Big Bang tell us not to steal? Does evolution tell us not to commit adultery? As far as marriage goes: what about the polygamist? Why would it be wrong for a man to marry three women? Conversely, why would it be wrong for a woman to marry three men and a woman? Since there is no longer an absolute standard, our society could end up allowing virtually anything.

What the homosexuals need to realize is that the very system that today may allow them to marry, if sentiments change in the future, could have them all jailed or killed. Once you leave morality up to the arbitrary whim of the masses, anything is possible.

So according to liberalism, we could some day have very Christian morals and viewpoints, or we could just as easily end up with a very Hitler-like outlook on the world. There is nothing stopping us from going in either direction. Of course, because of our Christian past, most people don't see us becoming excessively evil, but the point is, we have set up a system that allows for it, and no one can predict what will happen as a result. One thing that should be made clear is that anyone who gives consent to this system must take partial responsibility for whatever comes forth from it. This includes Christians who stand idly by, allowing it to happen.

It certainly was good to hear from you, and I must say your letter was very thought provoking. In answer to your question, I don't think there is any doubt you will do well in school. It can be a major transition, but if you work hard you will do well. Once you start doing well, you will gain the confidence you need to succeed. Good luck, and write again soon. I enjoy hearing from you.

With much love,
Uncle Greg

HOMOSEXUALITY

Dear Aaron,

Wow! I guess it didn't take you long to figure that out. At Penn State the homosexual agenda is pushed almost as soon as young freshmen step foot on campus, and I guess the same is true there. It's as if they believe world peace hinges on whether we accept homosexuality as morally equivalent with heterosexuality. What I really think is happening is that many white liberals are still feeling guilty over slavery and segregation, and they're scared to death they might end up on the wrong side of the next civil rights battle. They have picked the wrong side, by the way, on the abortion issue, but my guess is we will be discussing that at a latter date.

The difference between the civil rights movement of the '60s and the homosexual movement of today is that, on the one hand, the color of one's skin says nothing about the character or actions of the person, and so cannot be used as a means of judgment. On the other hand, homosexuality is something that one does, and therefore it can be judged. Even if the homosexual claims his homosexuality is something he is, and not simply something he does, what he is alluding to is a desire, and it also can be judged. For instance, according to Christianity we have been created to desire the opposite sex. So a desire for the same sex would be going against how God has created us to be, and would therefore be wrong.

I must say that the homosexual activists have been smart in aligning themselves with the civil rights movement. In doing so they have made many people afraid to judge their actions for fear of being labeled prejudiced or bigoted. You say you have already been labeled homophobic. If you continue to take a stand you will also be called a narrow-minded, right wing, hatemonger—and that's when they are being nice to you! I bet you never imagined you were so evil.

These labels are very effective in silencing debate, and that's the whole point. Since there really aren't any good arguments for homosexuality, the only remaining option is to silence those who are against it. After all, who wants to be labeled a bigot and a hatemonger? Most would rather remain quiet than to be looked down upon by their peers.

You have asked for some arguments to use when you enter into debate, and of course I'd be happy to provide you with some. I would just ask you to remember that your goal is to lead people to the truth through love. Believe me, I know, it's very easy to win an argument and lose the person. So be careful, and always check your motivations to make sure you are doing what you do for the right reasons.

That being said, the first and most obvious argument against homosexuality is biological. As I am sure you must know by now, men have a penis, and women have a vagina. From what I understand about the female body, which is just slightly more than I understand of the female mind, the vagina has two functions. One is for the penis to go in, and the other is for a baby to come out. We see from this that there is an opening in the female body that has been created specifically for the penis. As for the male, once he inserts his penis into the vagina, it becomes the instrument used to create a baby, who afterwards comes into the world through the same opening.

I think it's safe to say that for the average person, this short, sixth grade biology lesson is all the evidence necessary to show that men have been created to have sex with women. Homosexuals, of course, would not deny any of this. They would simply argue that they can find other creative ways of having sex, and that they are not limited to the strict biological method. This may be true, but what the biology shows is how we are created to be and that is what we are looking at here.

I think we can see this even more clearly if we look a little closer at the male and female bodies. As men, we know that we have many openings in our body, some of which a penis can fit into rather nicely, but none of which is made for that purpose. One would think that if we were to be having sex with each other, we would be equipped, not only with a penis, but also with a proper place to put it.

I think we can follow the same line of reasoning with the female body. Since the vagina was made for the penis, if women are supposed to be having sex with each other, then they should have come equipped with the proper instrument to put in to it, and they obviously did not.

It seems to me that anyone who studies human biology has to come to the conclusion that we have been created to be heterosexual. There is absolutely no biological evidence to the contrary. Therefore, I think this pretty clearly constitutes evidence number one, that we were created to be heterosexual and not homosexual.

The next evidence has to do with the purposes for sex, of which there are two. The first is the creation of life, which of course is something homosexuals cannot do. There is no need to spend time with this one since it is so obvious. It overlaps with the biological reasons and constitutes evidence number two as to why homosexuality is not the way we have been created to be.

The second purpose for sex is oneness. The male and female can be likened to two halves of a whole, and when they come together regularly, over years of a good marriage, they will eventually become one. Maybe you know of an elderly couple that not only have become inseparable, but also seem to know at all times what the other is thinking and feeling. As you may know, this oneness is not only an image of the relationship Christ wants with His Church, but it also binds the husband and wife together, making it harder for them to separate. This is evidenced by the nastiness and heartache of most divorces. This oneness gives the family, which is the basic building block of society, the best chance possible to survive.

Although some homosexuals claim to experience oneness in their relationship, it is at best a shadow of the real thing. For example, instead of putting a plug into a socket and creating electricity through the connection, they are attempting to put two plugs or two sockets together. They get closeness but never oneness. Even if they could become one, since they cannot be a family in the way God created it to be, then they cannot fulfill the purpose that He intended for the oneness He has created. In Christianity we do not believe that the end justifies the means.

I've tried my best to show you that homosexuality does not fulfill the biological, creation of life, or oneness aspects of sex. Hopefully it will help you, at least somewhat, in any future discussions. What I'd like to do now is proceed on to what I think are the two best arguments the homosexuals have, and consequently the ones you are most likely to hear. They will argue that they are born homosexual, and that they love one another.

The way they present the birth argument is that just as we were born heterosexual, they were born homosexual. They no more chose their sexual orientation than we did. In effect, they believe there is a gene or group of genes that makes one homosexual. First of all, Aaron, to this day there is no conclusive evidence for a homosexual gene, and secondly, as far as Christianity is concerned, it wouldn't matter if there were.

The question that needs to be asked is, does being born a certain way necessarily justify the corresponding behavior? I would say no, and use alcoholics as an example. You may be too young to remember this, but back in the '80s, and possibly in some circles today, it was popular to claim that some people were born alcoholics. Consequently, when they took their first drink, they were doomed to a life of drunkenness. The interesting thing is, as opposed to the arguments of homosexuals of today, they still confessed their behavior to be wrong and they attempted to change. Some were successful, and others were not, but what we can see by this example is that merely being born a certain way does not necessitate that the corresponding behavior is right.

The homosexuals' second argument is similar to the first. They make the claim that just as we love the opposite sex, they love the same sex. They don't choose who they fall in love with any more than we do. So how can we condemn their love just because it is oriented differently than ours? In response, we will ask a similar question as the one before, and that is, does being in love necessarily justify sex? Imagine if a 35-year-old son was having sex with his 65-year-old mother, and they were saying it was okay because they were in love. Hopefully most of us would see this as wrong and perverted despite their amorous claims. Obviously, simply being in love is not enough to justify sex. When we remember that homosexuality does not fulfill any of the purposes for sex, whether they are biological, creation of life, or oneness—any claim of love, or birthright—seems pretty hollow.

This also goes to the heart of the question of whether we should allow homosexuals to marry. If there is no evidence that homosexual sex is right, then how do we justify putting it on a par with heterosexual sex and allowing them the same privilege of marriage as the rest of us? The homosexuals should first have to prove that their sex is morally correct before we should even talk about marriages or civil unions. Remember, marriage is not a right guaranteed by the Constitution, but a privilege allotted by the states. If you meet the requirements, you are allowed the privilege.

It is also important to remember that, as Christians, we believe that man is fallen and far from perfect. Therefore, not all of our passions and desires are aligned correctly. We all have desires, even long standing ones, which we consider being wrong, and that need to be controlled. The homosexual's claim that because he has a desire his behavior must be right will never convince a Christian who understands the idea of being fallen. Neither should it convince anyone who has lived long enough to know that not every desire should be acted upon.

Hopefully this will give you and your adversaries something to think about. Try and keep in mind that even though as Christians we don't always love everything about someone—or ourselves for that matter—we are to see the image of God in him or her, and seek to love him as would Christ.

All the best,
Uncle Greg

— 4 —

HOMOSEXUAL ADOPTION

Dear Aaron,

I knew there was something I left out of my last e-mail, and I also knew you would remind me of it! You always were a sharp kid. I suppose the reason it slipped my mind was that adopting children, not to mention marriage, is a fairly new but not unexpected tactic taken up by the homosexual activists. Their strategy is to get as many institutions in America as possible to accept their behavior. The hope is that as successive generations come of age, they will be increasingly influenced by these institutions and therefore more willing to accept the homosexual agenda. As I said previously, their goal is not merely to have people put up with their behavior, but to see it as being morally equivalent with heterosexuality. This is why they will never be satisfied with civil unions. As long as they cannot be married in the same way as heterosexuals, they do not have full moral equality.

Now, of course, if one is against homosexuality one will be against homosexual adoption as well. Therefore, all the former arguments apply, but there are others we can look at that are specific to this issue. The claim that the homosexual activists make is that despite their sexual orientation, two loving people would be better for a child than for that child to be bounced around from foster home to foster home, oftentimes in abusive or less than ideal conditions.

I think we can grant the possibility that the foster care system may need to be revamped or replaced, but that does not justify redefining the family. Most people will agree that the ideal situation for children is to have a loving biological mother and a loving biological father. They not only bring the unique male and female perspective to the raising of the child, but also the examples for male and female roles: the boy will be able to learn what it is to be a man from his father, and how to treat a lady from his mother. Likewise, a young girl will be able to learn how to be a woman from her mother, and how to relate to a man from her father.

The importance of having biological parents is that they have the most invested in, and the closest ties to their children. They conceived their children through an act of love, and their kids will inherit many of their traits. They will look like their parents, walk like them, talk like them—and not only like them, but also like their grandparents, aunts, uncles, and cousins as well.

The question is what should be done when this ideal situation breaks down, and I think the answer is to try and approximate it as closely as possible. Adoption into a loving family would be one such option. Even a single parent family would be closer to the ideal than a homosexual one. In the case of the homosexual couple, we would be asking people to raise a life, even when these parents—in their most intimate and soul bearing moments—have denied life. It isn't that for one reason or another they have chosen not to create life; it's that homosexuality is a repudiation of life.

The Christian God is the God of life, and even though he can choose not to create if he wants, he never acts in a way that renounces life, and homosexuality by its very nature renounces life. In a similar way, the sexuality of a husband and wife who choose not to have children is not necessarily a renunciation of life. They have rightly or wrongly chosen not to create, but if they were to change their mind they could easily do so. The homosexual has no such choice.

The single-family household, amongst other expressions of family life, is broken. That will happen in a fallen world, but if it is fixed, life can result. Couples who for whatever reason cannot have children are the unfortunate victims of a breakdown in the created order, but if we had the proper technology we could fix it also. A homosexual household, on the other hand, cannot be fixed because it is other than what a family has been created to be.

Even if we were to grant that a homosexual couple could separate themselves from what their sexuality represents, and to one degree or another could love a child, the question is, do we want to put our kids into that sort of perverse, radically altered, life- denying environment? The Christian answer is a resounding no.

The thing to remember about the homosexual activist is that everything he does is to further the movement. He believes that if the movement is advanced both he and society will benefit. We, of course, believe that Christianity is the truth, and that furthering it will benefit society. As a people we will have to decide in which direction we wish to go.

I hope this answers your question. I'm glad to see you've jumped right into the fray. Far too many are content to sit on the sidelines hoping to make it through college— or life for that matter—unscathed. Neither Jesus, nor the Apostles, nor the great saints of the ages made it through life unscathed, and neither should we. If you're not bloody you're not in the battle, and if you're not in the battle, you are cheating your God, your church, your country, and yourself. So keep up the good work and keep in touch.

Love,
Uncle Greg

— 5 —
DATING

Dear Aaron,

Well, it didn't take long for that to happen. I was thinking after my last e-mail that I should have warned you of the attack to come. Whenever we as Christians get into the battle, Satan attacks, and he knows all of our weaknesses. Of course, there is no better way to trip up a young college guy than with sex.

So if I can sum up your e-mail, you've begun dating a beautiful young lady, to whom you are fiercely attracted, and you don't know whether you can control yourself. Believe me I understand, but before we go on, remember, Satan can ruin your testimony if he can ruin your character. It doesn't matter how much knowledge you possess; if you don't live the life, people will see you as a hypocrite and won't listen to what you have to say. So be prepared: this is where the devil will hit you over and over again. The struggle can be excruciatingly painful, and the battle fierce, but if you hang in there and don't give up, God will use it to purify you, and in the end you will be rewarded with Christ likeness.

Now as far as the girl goes, I think I am being true to the Christian perspective when I say that there is no reason to date someone unless you are thinking that at some future point you may want to marry her. So considering that she is not a Christian, there doesn't seem to be any reason for you to be dating her. That may sound harsh, and in your present state of infatuation almost impossible to believe, but marriage is difficult enough without attempting to blend two completely different worldviews.

One of the things that has greatly helped in my marriage to your Aunt is that since we are both Christian, we are in agreement on the important issues of life. There are enough problems to hammer out in marriage without coming into it from two very different understandings of the world.

Another aspect of this, which must be considered, is children. I realize kids are the furthest things from your mind right now, but they are the end result of the passion that is burning within you, and you would do well to keep that in mind. Most couples do have children, and I am sure you are going to want to bring yours up in the Christian faith. Imagine how confusing it would be for your kids to have parents of two different faiths. Many who find themselves in that situation either reject both religions, or create a strange amalgamation of the two, and I'm fairly certain neither of those options would appeal to you.

Even if for some reason you weren't going to have children, a Christian marriage is supposed to be a union of two souls and bodies, which are an image of the relationship between Christ and His Church. How can you possibly accomplish this with an unbeliever? My suggestion is, since the relationship is still in its infancy, keep it at a friendship level, and be more concerned about her soul than her body. If at some point in the future she has an honest conversion, then dating under the right conditions would be acceptable. Just keep in mind that dating is an exclusive relationship, and there is no reason to be exclusive with someone unless you are progressing towards marriage.

Even so, and even with a Christian girl, some precautions would be in order. First of all, since men are turned on sexually by sight, the woman should dress modestly so as to not unnecessarily add fuel to a fire that is sure to be already burning. The woman on the other hand is turned on primarily by touch. This is why the apostle Paul said it is better for a man not to touch a woman. The sexual act does not begin when the clothes come off, but with that first kiss or gentle touch. In other words, it is best not to start that which you are not planning to finish. There have been many young couples that have gotten into trouble thinking they could go part way and then stop. I don't know about women, but as guys, once we get started, everything in us screams to finish the job. So it's best not to start down that road.

Once you are married there will be plenty of time for sex. For now find a good Christian woman, and work on getting to know her. After all, the time spent having sex in marriage, while important, is miniscule compared to the time spent simply living together as partners. In the end, I think you'll find the latter to be more fulfilling than the former.

I hope this letter wasn't too harsh. I would just hate to see you go down the wrong road. You've got so much potential, but in the end the choice is yours to make. God seeks to woo you, but you are a sovereign person with a free will. I just hope you use it for the good, and not for indulging temporary passions. Please keep me apprised of the situation, and I will certainly be praying for you.

Your concerned uncle,
Uncle Greg

— 6 —

PREMARITAL SEX

Dear Aaron,

I see you are still struggling, and of course, I would be happy to provide you with more specific reasons as to why you should not have sex before you are married. Why they don't teach this during Sunday school or Youth Group I'll never know. I guess they don't want to upset the parents, but won't they be more upset if little Johnny comes home a parent himself?

Please understand, Aaron, that knowledge alone won't get you through this. It will take above all the grace of God and any will power you may have remaining. Keep in mind that Solomon was the wisest man who ever lived, and yet he fell through sexual temptation and marrying women of other faiths. So remember that knowledge is important, but without the grace of God we would all fall.

I think the best place to begin this discussion is where we began the one on homosexuality, and that involved the reasons for the existence of sex. Once we are clear as to why sex has been created, then we can look at your situation and see whether you would be fulfilling God's creative purpose by engaging in it at this time.

As I said in our discussion on homosexuality, there are two reasons for sex, the first of which is to create life. I think we can agree that as an unmarried college student you are not ready for that responsibility. So there is really no sense in discussing it any further. The other, if you remember, is to become one with your partner. Even though the process of becoming one begins the first time you have sex, it takes a lifetime to bring it to fulfillment. I think we all know that most sexual relationships at the college level are lucky to last a year. Since this is barely enough time to get to know each other, I don't think it meets the criteria for becoming one.

In passing, I guess I should mention that pleasure is not one of the reasons that sex has been created. In my opinion, if the sexual act were not pleasurable it would be a rather strange thing to do. Who would take the time and effort? Therefore it is pleasurable so we will do it frequently, create life, and become one. Pleasure may be a motivator, and is definitely an effect, but it is not one of the reasons for the existence of sex. So if we can agree that oneness and the creation of life are the reasons for sex, and that they are best accomplished in a committed lifelong relationship, then I think we can conclude that no sex outside of marriage, much less that done amongst college students, fulfills God's creative purpose.

The interesting thing to me is that the most common objection I hear from the heterosexual students at Penn State is the same one I hear from the homosexual students, and that is that they love one another. The problem is, when I ask them to define love for me, what I usually get in return is a somewhat incoherent response that finally ends with them complaining about how hard it is to put emotions and feelings into words. In essence, what they are doing is justifying a behavior using a word they cannot define. They may as well be saying, "Sex before marriage is good because of *oogbla*."

Just in case you may be having similar problems, let me define the word for you, and we'll see if the actions you may be contemplating are consistent with the definition. I think a reasonable Christian definition of love, would be to act in another's highest good, even if it would mean the sacrifice of one's self. If you agree with this definition and the reasons for sex outlined above, ask yourself if it would be in your girlfriend's best interest to have sex with you now or her husband later. I think the answer is obvious. If you agree, then I think it is equally as obvious that your motivation for having sex with her is born out of selfishness and lust, and not out of love.

It seems as if you've made the classic mistake of confusing infatuation with love. Infatuation is when you meet someone and the skyrockets go off, and you think you've met the first goddess to ever walk the earth. You'll write her name over and over in a notebook just to gaze upon it. You will stand outside in the pouring rain and not even care as long as she is with you. Even her faults endear her to you. Sound familiar?

Don't be mistaken, there is nothing wrong with any of this; in fact, it is necessary to initially attract you to somebody, but it is not yet love. At least it is not yet the type of love needed to justify sexual relations. True love comes when the infatuation wears off, her faults irritate you, and standing outside in the rain seems absurd, but in spite of all this you make the decision to stay with her, and act to her highest good for the rest of your life. I know this doesn't sound very romantic, but it will get you through the hard times when romance will not.

All of the above being said, what I'd like to do now is to take a moment and go over something you are likely to hear from some of your less than Christian friends and dorm mates. One excuse I've heard from the guys at Penn State is that they want to have sex *now*, so that when they get married they will know how to satisfy their wives. Not only is this insulting to women, making them the scrub team upon whom the first team is practicing, but it is also a fundamental misunderstanding of sex.

Having sex is not just about using the body in various ways. Past experiences, moods, likes, dislikes, personality, and even the slightly different way each body reacts all comes into play. So what these guys need to learn is that having sex with their girlfriends today will not be the same as having sex with their wives later. The only way to learn to please your wife is to get married and have years of sexual relations with her. Far from getting boring, as some guys will tell you, practice as usual makes perfect. After a while you will know things about your mate and ways of pleasing her that you could have never known the first time. All things being equal, sex after thirty years will be deeper, richer, and more pleasurable than it ever could have been at the beginning.

The next bit of advice I usually save for women, but I'll give it to you anyway, and if you can't use it maybe you'll run into a young lady some day who can. It's not that it can't apply to a guy, but it has to do with relationship, and my experience is that for most guys when it comes to sex, especially premarital sex, relationship is nice but not necessary. Guys tend to be more focused on accomplishing the act than furthering the relationship. Most women, on the other hand, need to at least believe that there is a real, loving, relationship involved when they are having sex.

The problem is, when you are a single girl, it is often hard to tell whether a guy loves you or just loves having sex with you. The only way I know of to find out for sure is for her to let him know that she will not be having any more sex until she is married. If she does this, remains strong, and sticks with it, one of two things will happen. He will either leave her, and in that case there was no reason for the two to be having sex to begin with, or he will stay and eventually marry her, and in that way prove his love for her in the best way he can.

There are other reasons for not being sexually active before marriage such as the possibility of contracting a sexual disease, or running into a former sexual partner once you are married, which always goes over well with one's spouse. Even having the assurance that you are the best sexual partner that your mate has ever had can make a world of difference in a marriage, but I think you get the point. There are simply no good reasons to engage in premarital sex, and many reasons not to.

What you and your friends need to decide is whether you are going to follow your head or your hormones: your mind or your passions. It is my belief that if we can control our appetite for sex and for food, then we can control all others, because they are the ones that scream at us the loudest. I'll admit that I still struggle with these and with others, but I've made the decision to struggle, and if I fall, I've made the decision to get back up and continue on towards the goal.

Your decision on this issue could well affect the rest of your life. As I said earlier, I am praying for you, but the decision is yours. It is so important to understand that God will prod, encourage, and help you, but he will not take over your will. Please keep me informed, and do not be afraid to let me know what you decide. I'll hang in there with you no matter what.

Continuing to pray for you,
Uncle Greg

MASTURBATION

D ear Aaron,

Well I must admit I didn't think of that as a solution, but I understand why you would. The common joke is that 98% of guys admit to masturbating, and the other 2% are lying. I don't know if that is true, but I certainly suspect that it is. As a result, many in this day and age, including many pastors, are seeking to justify masturbation as an alternative to premarital sex.

Your friends are certainly correct when they tell you that there are no specific scriptures against masturbating, but Jesus did say that if you lust in your heart, you are just as guilty as if you had already committed the act. The reason for this is that since your character is known outwardly by your actions, and inwardly by your thoughts and desires, it is just as tainted, whether you do something openly or desire it secretly. God, of course, knows the heart, and it is the heart he is seeking to change. Although some may claim that they can masturbate without lusting, it is always lust that directs them to do it. Even if some of your friends insist otherwise, it is obviously so in your case.

Another, and maybe more important point, is that of self-control. You would not be exercising any more self-control if you masturbated, than if you were to have sex with your girlfriend. You may have a point that there would be less physical, and maybe even spiritual consequences, but there would be consequences nonetheless. One such consequence is that you would become less Christ like and more animals like. Remember, we were created to become like Christ, and our animal like condition is a result of the fall. Animals have sex/masturbate whenever they get the urge. We as humans can exercise self-control, which raises us above the animals, and closer to Christ. Salvation is the process of becoming Christ like, and we can judge our actions by whether or not they lead us in that direction.

Another physical, but still important reason, is that masturbation causes us to focus on ourselves during the sexual act. Most don't make the connection, but in my view, this is one of the reasons why many women do not enjoy sex even after they are married. After ten to twenty years of masturbating, most guys have trained themselves to think first and foremost about their own satisfaction while having sex. Many never make the transition to satisfying their wives, and therefore, many women are left sexually unfulfilled.

Look, Aaron, I know that it's difficult, and you are right, I wasn't a Christian in college, and I certainly did not exercise much in the way of self-control. I have seen both sides though, and can tell you from experience, that the paths you are contemplating lead only to corruption and heartache. Of course, you are right, if you choose the wrong path, you can repent and God will forgive you, but you will carry those scars with you for the rest of your life. Take it from someone who knows—it's not worth it. Choose wisely. You and those in your future will be glad that you did.

Still concerned,
Uncle Greg

CONDOM USE

Dear Aaron,

You certainly are going at this from every possible angle. I must say I admire your persistence. I only wish it was taking you in the right direction. I'd be tempted to blame all of this on the advice you seem to be getting from your friends, but I've never allowed my kids to get away with that, so I guess I won't start now with you.

It seems as if in your infatuated, hormone-charged state, you've forgotten all about your Christianity. I will most certainly tell you why I don't believe that condoms are the answer for you, or anyone else for that matter, but in the meantime, maybe you should ask yourself how you got to the point where you even have to pose the question.

I do realize that at universities condoms are being pushed as the cure for all our sexual ills. There have been days at Penn State when students have actually given them away right in front of the Willard Building where I preach. Some can't understand why I am so against what they are trying to do, since they claim that condoms will not only reduce the instances of sexual disease, but will also lower the abortion rate. What I try to show them is that condoms have been pushed as a solution to these problems since the '60s, and all these years later, we still have a million to a million and a half abortions a year, and we actually have more sexual diseases now then we did then.

Back in the '70s, when I was young, all we had to be concerned about was gonorrhea and syphilis, and they were easily curable. Today there are so many sexual diseases that I can't keep track of them all. Some of them are incurable; others are deadly. How many years will we push the same solution before we admit that it doesn't work? Do we honestly believe that if condoms haven't worked in all these years, if we wait another five they will?

Without further delay, let me try and give you some reasons why, at least on the college campus, condoms are not the answer. These may or may not pertain directly to you, but they are part of the sexual culture with which you seem to want to align yourself. Besides, I have confidence that one day the clouds will part, and you will see clearly once more. At that time, some of this information may come in handy.

First of all, guys have known from the beginning of time that it is easier to obtain sex with a woman if she is drunk than if she is sober. If the truth were known, the primary reason for alcohol on a college campus is to prime the pump for sexual encounters. This is both the main reason for pushing condoms and the main reason for their failure.

One problem is that most guys, for all their bluster, don't really believe that they are actually going to have sex on any particular weekend. Even if some do, they are oftentimes too embarrassed to pick up a condom, despite the fact that most universities are doing everything they can to get them into their hands. In addition, most women, unless they already have a steady boyfriend, won't carry a condom with them for fear of appearing to be a whore ready to have sex with the first guy she meets.

Most unprotected sex is not done in "long term relationships," which I admit is a bit of an oxymoron on a college campus, but in casual hookups that are being fueled by alcohol and hormones. This is anything but conducive to clear thinking and cautious behavior.

Even if a guy does happen to have a condom with him during one of these encounters, the chances of him actually using it are slim. A typical scenario would have a guy and a girl who know each other on some level running into one another at a party. They are both intoxicated, and as the night progresses they become more and more sexually attracted to each other. One thing leads to another, and they find themselves in bed about ready to engage in intercourse. At that moment, how many guys in their intoxicated, hormone-charged state will stop everything, rifle through their pants, find their wallet, fish out the condom, open it up, put it on, and only then finish the deed? For most guys in that state, putting on a condom is the furthest thing from their mind.

Even if the thought does occur to them, most would be scared to death to stop the process, for fear that if the girl has a few moments to think, she might begin wondering what she is doing in bed with a guy she barely knows. At that point she may begin having second thoughts, and possibly shut the whole thing down. This, as we all know, is every guy's worst and most painful nightmare. You see, the real reason condoms will never be effective in preventing sexual diseases and unwanted pregnancies is that the situation in which they are most needed is that in which human nature is least inclined to use them.

Besides, Aaron, the real reason we have a problem with unwanted pregnancies and sexual diseases is not the lack of wearing a condom, but in engaging in sex before marriage. For instance, if your Aunt and I were to engage in sexual relations tonight (sorry about the visual) we would not have to wear a condom to protect us from disease, and our relationship is such that children are welcome. On the other hand, if I went out to the bars tonight, and picked up someone at two in the morning, I'd better be wearing something to protect myself. The problem is, we don't want to control ourselves, but neither do we want to bear the consequences of our actions.

I've tried to relate some of these ideas to those who are pushing condoms at Penn State, but they normally aren't too inclined to accept them. Not only have condoms become part of the popular wisdom of our day, but also abstinence, which is the only real alternative, is unthinkable to most of them.

Anytime anyone begins to publicly proclaim abstinence, he or she immediately gets shot down and are told that it is unrealistic to expect young people in this day and age to control themselves. Proponents are considered to be out of touch and devoid of love for even considering such an idea. On the contrary, it seems to me that those who would say that it is unrealistic for young people to control themselves are disrespecting these young men and women, seeing them as little more than dogs in heat.

Human beings can control themselves. Dogs, on the other hand, once they come into heat, simply jump the nearest dog they can find.

Contrary to what we are told, the ones who uphold a reasonably high standard have more respect and love for those they are addressing than they who have the lower standard. As Christians, we believe that human beings have the ability to overcome desires that may be harmful to them, and to choose what is right. Even if those who oppose us believed that sex before marriage was wrong, they still wouldn't believe that we could do anything about it other than try and protect ourselves from the inevitable consequences.

One final point I'd like to make is that there are those who say that it is futile for parents to talk to their kids about sex. They tell us that teenagers are naturally rebellious, and they will do the opposite of what they are told. Why these same people are pleading with us to talk to our kids about drugs is anybody's guess. You would think the hypocrisy would be obvious. Be that as it may, if their theory were correct, we should certainly refrain from telling our kids not to murder, rape, or steal, because as soon as we do, they will immediately run out and become criminals.

Why is sex the only thing we shouldn't be teaching our kids to abstain from, and expecting them to do as we say? I think it's because my generation began the sexual revolution, and we don't want to repudiate that which was such a fundamental part of who we were and to a large degree are still. We were rebellious, and so we assume our kids will be rebellious also. Therefore, the best we think we can do is to find some way of protecting them.

Aaron, I urge you not to fall into this trap. I know it sounds good, but even if condoms could save you from some of the physical consequences of your behavior, and that is far from certain, what about the spiritual ones? What is going to save you from them? I have yet to hear of the spiritual equivalent of the condom.

Very much concerned,
Uncle Greg

0004500093

**Sell your books at
sellbackyourBook.com!**
Go to sellbackyourBook.com
and get an instant price
quote. We even pay the
shipping - see what your old
books are worth today!

— 9 —
ABORTION

Dear Aaron,

So, you discovered that your girlfriend is pro-choice. Is that really so surprising given today's culture and her sexual proclivities? Although there are more who consider themselves to be pro-life today than there were when I first began evangelizing in the early '80s, you will still find that at least one out of two people will identify himself to be pro-choice. Also, it should not surprise you that her arguments tend to be emotional in nature. This is not because she is a woman (as you alluded to), but since the facts are on our side, emotion is all she has. I would be happy to help you in your discussions, but don't hold your breath. From what you've told me she seems pretty entrenched in this one.

Since you say you had a fairly long and heated discussion, then I am sure one of the arguments she proposed was that she has a right to do whatever she wants with her own body. But does she? Do not the laws against drug use, prostitution, and even suicide in most states clearly show us that we do not have the right to do anything we wish with our body? Plus, I think the very idea that the baby is a part of the mother's body is foolish at best. It is definitely attached to and drawing nutrients from the mother, but its genetic makeup is different. It has the mother's, but also the father's DNA, and since its genes are consistent with that of being human, the only rational conclusion is that the fetus is a human being who has come from the mother and the father, but still has its own unique identity.

This is sixth grade biology, and maybe seventh grade civics, so why is it so hard for us to accept? The answer goes back to my first e-mail.

Remember when I wrote that my generation's philosophy of life was to have pleasure without responsibility? Well, abortion is all about the desire to have sex without responsibility. All of our talk of civil rights is just a smokescreen for a hedonistic lifestyle. Yes, I know, abortion is supposedly a constitutional right, but so was slavery. We should all realize by now that just because something is civilly right doesn't mean necessarily that it is morally right.

Of course, those who are pro-choice will tell you that there is no comparison between abortion and slavery, but the connection is that both are justified using a philosophy of dehumanization. In the case of slavery, the African was thought to be more animal than human. As a result, he could be bought, sold, worked in the field, and even beaten and killed, as an animal. As far as abortion goes, the baby in the womb is said to be only potentially human and therefore can be disposed of without any moral qualms. In both cases the subject has been dehumanized.

In light of this, ask your girlfriend if she can name one instance since the world began that when a government has declared some portion of its population to be less human than the rest, history has proved them to be right. If she can think of one let me know, because I cannot. It appears as if—at least in this case—history is on our side.

Besides, if we as Americans value human rights as I believe we do, and if we are not sure when life begins, as we say we aren't, don't you think the humane thing to do would be to put a moratorium on abortion until we are sure? I guess that's more of a question for your girlfriend than for you. I must say though that this whole line of reasoning frustrates me. Essentially what we are saying is that we do not know when human life begins, so let's continue a potentially deadly practice until we do. Shouldn't we be assuming that the fetus is human until it can be definitively proven otherwise? If not, we may wake up one day and realize that for decades we have killed a million to a million and a half babies a year, just so we can have sex without consequences. Our insatiable desire for pleasure has darkened our reasoning.

Let me move on to what I believe is the best argument that the other side has to offer. I'm sure you heard some variant of it in your discussion the other night. The gist of it is that the embryo is not fully human because human beings have a heart and a brain and the embryo does not.

The most important thing to understand is that this argument deals with how far along in its development the baby is and not how human it is. If it wasn't fully human at conception, then we should be able to find something that enters into the egg after fertilization that completes its humanity, and as far as I know we have not. In addition, the embryo not only has human DNA, and is developing all of its various parts, but it is also the product of a human mother, a human father, a human sperm, and a human egg. If everything about it is human, why are we judging it based on its level of development? Isn't it the basis of all genocide to judge a people unworthy of life because they don't measure up to an arbitrary standard laid down by the powerful? Haven't we as Americans always fought against that sort of thing?

Also, if we are going to decide how human we are based on our stage of development, I could make the argument that newborn babies are not fully human. Following the reasoning of those who are for abortion, I would simply make the point that since a newborn child cannot walk, talk, or reason on a level higher than an animal, then it must be something less than entirely human. Any thinking person would reject this argument because he would know that if left alone, a baby who matures normally would develop these abilities. It just needs time. I would make the same point about the embryo. If left alone, and given time, it will be just like us, as we were at one time just like it. The embryo doesn't become human as it develops. It develops as it does because it is human.

By the way, I am sure you have heard people say that they are personally against abortion, but they do not feel that they have a right to tell someone else what to do. Next time you hear someone say that ask him why he is opposed to abortion. There is, of course, only one reason, and that is because they think it is the killing of a human being. If this is the case, then they not only have the right, but the obligation to speak out.

Well, Aaron, good luck. I sincerely hope you can convince her to change her mind. One final suggestion, if I may. If she gets frustrated and tells you that you cannot speak on this issue because you are not a woman and cannot get pregnant, tell her that as a former fetus you are against abortion, and that you are speaking up on behalf of all your brothers and sisters who are still in the womb. Gets 'em every time.

Yours truly,
Uncle Greg

— 10 —

FEMINISM

Dear Aaron,

I can't say I'm surprised, not to mention relieved, that the relationship has ended. At first the suddenness of it struck me, but as you said, there was a battle raging within you the whole time. I'm just thankful that the right side has won. As I said, it is hard to meld two completely different worldviews, especially when they are held as strongly as were the two of yours. I do hope you can remain friends, and I must say I am a bit shocked you didn't realize that she is a feminist. The power of infatuation never ceases to amaze me.

Personally, it is only the radical feminists that bother me, and that is because I think their agenda is harmful to society. One of the most harmful causes our local feminists push for is typified by the slogan "Yes means yes and no means no." In other words, they believe that no matter where a woman is, who she is with, or in whatever state of sexual involvement she happens to be, if she says no all activity must cease. Now maybe if we lived in a feminized version of an ideal world this would work, but we don't, and many young women have been raped as a result.

If we keep in mind that once a guy begins the sexual act everything in him screams to finish the job, I'll walk you through a typical date rape scenario. Two students, much like the ones we talked about earlier, have hooked up after a night of drinking and dancing. One thing leads to another, and they are just about ready to engage in intercourse, when the young woman begins to have second thoughts. Maybe he stopped a bit too long to find his condom before resuming action. At any rate, it's a little late in the process, but being well schooled in feminist thought, she tells him that she is ready to stop. The guy in his inebriated male mind cannot think of one reason to have gone that far only to pack his bags and go home. He hears her say no, and yet everything in him screams go. In his drunken state he obeys his passions and forces his way through. Now she has been raped, and he may be going to jail, and all because of a misguided feminist slogan.

I think feminists would help women a lot more if they would encourage them not to start what they aren't planning to finish. This may cut back on what they perceive to be feminist freedoms and ideals, but it will keep many women from being raped, and many men from becoming rapists.

It has also been my observation over the years that far from sexually empowering women, feminism has actually weakened them. It all began on a positive note in the late '60s when the feminists began to decry the sexual double standard that existed in America. In those days it was considered to be okay for a young man to sow his wild oats. In fact, his peers for doing so admired him, but if a woman was sexually active before marriage she was considered to be a whore. This was obviously wrong, and the feminists had a golden opportunity to raise the standard. They could have declared, "If we are considered to be whores if we have sex before marriage, and if you won't marry us if we do, then we will consider you to be whoremongers and won't marry you if you do." Sadly, Instead of taking the high road, they took the low one, and in essence said that it was okay for them to sow their wild oats too. In my opinion women have been paying the price ever since.

You see, the power a woman used to have was that when a guy was pursuing her and desiring sex, she made him prove his love first by taking responsibility and marrying her. These days as soon as a woman feels a certain way towards a guy, and he claims to love her, she gives him everything. As I assume you know, under these circumstances most guys will take everything but won't really respect the women who give it. I've heard many women complain that it's hard these days to get men to commit to marriage, but why should they? As grandma used to say, "Why buy the cow if you can get the milk for free?"

I can't help but believe that most of the feminist movement today is simply women wanting to be men and losing what it is to be a woman in the process. Not only do feminists want to be sexually promiscuous like men, but I am also convinced that knowing there were more consequences for them than for us, they saw abortion as a way of leveling the playing field. In the process they learned to despise the fruit of their womb. Many of them want careers like men, and as a result are losing their motherhood. Some even dress like men and sport male haircuts, seemingly despising their femininity.

On the one hand, much of this only applies to the more radical feminists, but on the other hand, most feminists, and dare I say most Americans today, have been influenced to some degree by this philosophy. Your ex sounds as if she has been influenced more than most, but remember you are planting seeds now that may come to fruition years from now. So keep up the good work, and try not to get too frustrated. Who knows, she may end up thanking you in the end.

Much relieved,
Uncle Greg

11

MALE/FEMALE ROLES

D ear Aaron,

You ask a very good but controversial question. One that is certain to get you into trouble. As you are sure to find out, even the mention of differing roles for men and women is enough to give most feminists fits. The reason for this is that it doesn't fit into their view of equality between the sexes. As far as I understand the Christian tradition, these roles only apply in the home and in the Church, but even that is too much for most feminists.

If you remember the Biblical account of creation, God first made man, and then from man, fashioned the woman to be a helpmate for him. You'll notice I said helpmate not slave. They were to walk side by side in the garden, taking care of, and ruling over, the creation. Unfortunately the fall changed everything. Once sin entered the world and there was no longer harmony between Adam and Eve, God had to designate someone to lead. Since Adam was created first, with Eve as his helper, he was given that authority. Once again this was not as a master ruling over his slave, but as a king with his queen.

The problem with giving both partners equal authority in a fallen world is that you will always have a power struggle. If no one is designated to lead, there will always be competition to see who will make the next decision, as well as scorekeeping as to who made the last. Now if both partners are Christian, which would be the ideal, they will already have a basic agreement on many issues, and hopefully a willingness to compromise on many others. Of course, as we are all very much aware, there will inevitably be those times when no compromise can be reached, and that is when the man has been designated to make the final decision. Hopefully, he fully understands and appreciates his wife's position, and through much prayer and contemplation he makes a wise choice.

This is the ideal, and I will freely admit that none of us do it perfectly, but it is surely better than the feminist model, which produces only argument and strife. The evidence for this can be found in how the divorce rate has skyrocketed since the 1970s when feminism first began to take hold in America. It may not be the only reason for this increase, but in my opinion, it is certainly a major factor.

Now as far as the exact roles that the husband and wife should play, I think this needs to be worked out between them, depending upon the strengths and weaknesses of each. There is an exception though, and that is, if at all possible the man should work to supply for his family, and the woman should be the primary nurturer of the children. This does not mean that the wife cannot work, or that the father should not nurture. As long as the primary roles are understood and followed as much as possible, some crossing over is natural and good. I know this gives feminists fits and may get you slapped if you say it, but I believe that this is not only consistent with traditional Christianity, but is also consistent with who we are as men and women.

As men, we get much of our self worth and identity from our work. We were created to provide for and to protect our families, and if you take that away, you take away a good part of what it is to be a man. As for women, they begin bonding with their baby even while it is in the womb, which is obviously something men cannot do. After nine months of bonding she gives birth, and then through her breasts continues to give life to her baby, making that bond even stronger. Because of this, I believe that God has given women a more highly developed nurturing instinct than He has men. Consequently, I believe it hurts a woman more than it does a man to be separated from her children.

The feminist response to all of this is to show exceptions to the rule, but they will be just that, exceptions, not the rule. When we speak of human nature, especially in our fallen state, there will always be exceptions. We just shouldn't pretend that they are the norm and make public policy from them.

As far as the Church goes, God has always chosen to identify Himself to us as a male. He also chose men to be priests under the old covenant. When the Trinity was revealed, we were told that God had an only begotten Son, Who when He became incarnate, did so as a man. He then chose twelve men to be his disciples. When they set up the Church they chose male bishops, priests, and deacons.

The bishop, or at his behest the priest, represents Christ to the Church, which is called his bride. If you have a woman as bishop or priest, you are not only representing Christ as a female, but you are then marrying her to her bride the Church, thereby creating a female deity, and a lesbian relationship! Assuming that theological ideas have consequences, is it any wonder that many of the denominations that allow female pastors also seek to accept homosexuality and make God gender neutral, or even worse, a goddess? In my opinion, it is goddess worship that is the ultimate goal for most of the radical feminists.

I believe another reason why God has chosen to reveal Himself as a male, is that since he made man the authority in marriage, and then reveals himself to be in a marriage relationship with his Church, if he revealed Himself as a female, we wouldn't view him as the authority figure. If he revealed Himself as gender neutral we wouldn't see him as a personal God.

My generation may be a lost cause, but maybe yours will understand that differing roles do not necessarily mean inequality. They are meant to complement one another so the two may become one. Men and women were never meant to fight and compete with each other, but to be as one throughout eternity. What we as Americans have to decide is whether modern day feminism, or

Christianity, is more likely to get us to that goal. It is up to us to make the case for Christianity as well as we can, and then let people decide for themselves.

Your loving uncle,
Greg

12

EVIDENCES FOR
THE EXISTENCE OF GOD

D ear Aaron,

I think it's great that your fellowship is going to be evangelizing on campus. Far too many campus groups end up being merely a social club where Christians can gather to encourage each other and eat ice cream. Please don't misunderstand; I think the social aspect of Christianity is wonderful. Community is a huge part of our religion, and many married Christian couples first met at a church or fellowship meeting. I don't know if you are aware of it, but your Aunt and I got to know each other through one such campus fellowship.

My initial cynicism comes from years of seeing these groups wither away the opportunity of a lifetime to evangelize people from all over the country and the world. They often times seem to be more concerned with being accepted by the darkness than with being a light in the midst of it. It seems as if their fear of being thought of as ignorant and foolish is greater than their desire to rescue souls. Nevertheless, I am overjoyed that you will be venturing out into the harvest, and hopefully something I say here will be helpful.

I think the best way to help you get started is to give some evidences for the existence of God. If you run into difficulties in other areas please let me know, but I think this will be a good place to begin. Universities continue to be one of the few places in America where you will find an inordinate number of atheists.

One thing you will discover is that atheists enjoy seeing themselves as part of the intellectual elite. They fancy themselves to have seen the world through the cold, hard eyes of reason, and in doing so have discovered that there is no God. We, the masses who believe in God, are considered to be poor ignorant peasants who rely on emotion and superstition to get us through our miserable lives.

On the contrary, it is atheism that is always emotional. It is never based on reason. The easiest way for this to be shown is to ask the atheist how he knows that there is no God. Since we are all ignorant of most of the knowledge available in the universe, much less any which may be available in the spiritual world, the atheist has no way of knowing whether part of his ignorance is actually the knowledge of God. It is possible to know that God exists, as he can choose to reveal himself to us, but it is impossible to know that he does not exist, because we cannot prove the negative. Since there is not an intellectual way to know that God does not exist, then all atheism must be based on emotionalism.

In light of this, I think there are a few basic reasons why certain people choose to become atheists. For some it is because of a tragedy that happened at some point in their life, for which they either blame God, or cannot reconcile with the existence of a loving God. These tend to be the angry atheists. Others, as they came into adolescence, became aware of hypocrites within the Church and got turned off to religion because of them. These tend to be the cynical ones. Still others have a lot of pride in their intelligence and abilities and in essence, desire to be their own God. These will tend to be arrogant and condescending and commonly found at universities.

One thing virtually all atheists will have in common is a belief in evolution. They think they have found a way for the universe to come about on its own so that there is no need for God. Obviously you have learned about evolution during your time in the public schools. I assume you have figured out that, although it is a popular theory with all the force of modern science behind it, in the end, it is simply the belief that everything came about by chance over a long period of time. Evolutionists hate to hear it put that way because it sounds so simplistic, but nonetheless that is the essence of what they believe.

Now what do you think are the odds, of everything in the universe, including intelligent life, happening by chance? I would say they are astronomical at best. If we were to take anything that has complexity, order, and usefulness, even something as simple as a chain link fence, does anyone really believe that given enough time, random events could bring it about? As another example, imagine that we put all the parts of a bicycle in a weightless environment, magnetized them to attract each other, and left them there indefinitely. What would be the odds that at some point we would find a fully functioning bike? Again, I think they would be astronomical. What if we did this an infinite amount of times? What would the odds be that we would ever get anything more than a random conglomeration of parts? Once again they would be enormous, but this is where the evolutionists have put their faith. They believe that given enough time anything can happen. It takes just as much—if not more faith—to believe this than it does to believe in a creator. I don't think any of us really believe that we could get something as simple as a bike or a chain link fence by chance. How in the world do we think we could get a fully functioning universe with intelligent life?

Even if we were to assume that evolution was true, it still would not mean that there is no God. Science can neither prove nor disprove the existence of God. If evolution were true, there could still be a god in heaven watching it all unfold. In the end, I believe it is simply human nature—when we look at something that has complexity, order, and usefulness—that we assume a creator, and if we weren't educated otherwise we would do the same with the universe.

Another evidence for the existence of God is that in every society that anthropologists unearth, there is resident in that society a belief in the supernatural. I think it is safe to assume that if God did not exist, a belief in the supernatural would take some time to evolve. One could very easily postulate that for many thousands of years there would be no evidence for God in human society. After a while we would discover some simple expressions of worship and eventually more complex ones. What we find though, is complex religious ritual in even the most primitive societies. This seems to be more consistent with a God who has created us with an innate understanding of Him—and our expressing that understanding through worship—than it does of us evolving in a Godless world, and yet somehow still having an instinct to believe.

I'm sure you will encounter some who will argue that when primitive man saw things he could not understand, such as lightning, volcanic eruptions, eclipses, etc. that his easiest and simplest response would have been to claim that it was the work of a supernatural being. I would have to disagree. It seems to me that the easiest response would have been for him to declare his ignorance and fear of such phenomenon, and in the case of lightning run back into his cave for cover. If he did feel the need to explain these events, he could have chalked them up to natural forces, and then at some point begun the process of trying to understand them.

Certainly, creating a God with particular characteristics, commandments to follow, and prescriptions for worship, would not have been his simplest response. Even if he did believe that God was behind these events, it would merely show how natural it is for us to believe in Him. In my opinion, this would actually be evidence for the existence of God, and our innate knowledge of Him.

This next bit of evidence is slightly more complex, but being the bright young man that you are, I am sure that you will be able to grasp it easily enough. It seems to me that it is natural for us as humans to have objective morals. By this I mean we all hold certain actions to be right or wrong, not just for ourselves, which would be subjective morality, but for everyone, which is objective morality. The specifics may vary from person to person, as one may believe murder to be wrong for all, and another rape, and yet another eating too many peas on Sunday. What they all have in common, though, is the belief that there are some things that are right or wrong for everyone, despite one's personal beliefs to the contrary.

Philosophically this is only possible if there is a God. To understand this, let us imagine that there is no God, and we all crawled out of the primordial slime, and are now nothing more than glorified slime balls. Who then has the authority to set the moral standard for everyone else? We are all fallible human beings. There is not a superior class who inherently has a greater moral authority than the rest. Of course, societies for what they believe to be their highest good can create laws and punish those who break them, but this is not an objective moral authority. It is merely that which is born of force and the changing opinion of the masses, and we all know that this can be highly unreliable and dangerous. One only has to think of slavery to understand what can happen when we allow public opinion to dictate morality.

The obvious point here is that if there is no God, all morality is merely human opinion, and there are no absolutes. On the other hand, if there is a God who is the creator, omniscient, and perfectly good, he can reveal how he created man to live, and anyone who acts differently would be wrong, independent of his personal beliefs. God's commands are objective and absolute, and that is how man thinks and lives. If you need an example of this, imagine seeing a woman being raped. Would your first thought be, "Well that would be wrong for me, but I don't know about him," or would it be, "He's doing something wrong, and I must stop him." You see how it is human nature to declare a universal morality and act upon it. This is perfectly consistent with the existence of a God Who has created us to act in certain ways, and not at all consistent with a humanity floating all alone in the universe free to do as it pleases.

Finally, as human beings we all believe that there is a purpose and meaning to life. None of us can go through our daily lives without believing that there is some reason for it. We may not all ascribe to it a supernatural meaning, but we all ascribe meaning nonetheless. The problem is, if there is no God there is no meaning. We are simply an accident in a universe of accidents, and one day when the sun is extinguished, and life on earth ends, there will be no more remembrance of anyone or anything. Who could live his life believing that nothing he does has any ultimate purpose, without falling into a deep depression? Even atheists ascribe some reason or purpose to life; otherwise, they could not go on.

On the other hand, if there is a God, then He is the reason for our existence. This not only explains our innate sense that life has meaning, but it also fulfills it. As you know, the meaning to life is not a thing but a person—a person with whom we can have a relationship, a person who can fulfill us.

In closing I'd like to point out that all of these evidences flow directly out of human nature, and how we naturally think and act. Therefore I believe that they will make the biggest impression on any atheists or agnostics you may encounter. Let me know how it goes, and if you run into any questions you can't answer, drop me a line. If I don't have the answer I'm sure I know somebody who does.

All the best,
Uncle Greg

— 13 —
DRUNKENNESS AND
CONFORMITY OF THOUGHT

Dear Aaron,

It really should not surprise you that all of a sudden, your roommate is getting more and more into the party scene and that he even wants his girlfriend to sleep over. You'll notice that this is happening shortly after you made the commitment to evangelize with your fellowship. It is the Devil's way of getting back at you. In his mind you are messing with him, so he is going to mess with you. What I would do, in a nice way, is tell your roommate that what he does on his own time is up to him, but that you'd appreciate it if the room were a party and sex-free zone. I was quite a partier in college, and even though I may not have liked such an arrangement, I would have respected it, and hopefully your roommate will also.

As to why your roommate, and so many others on college campuses get drunk, there are the obvious reasons, such as having fun, relieving stress, and finding women, but I believe that these are the symptoms and not the cause. I think the real reason is simply peer pressure. The first thing an eighteen year old who is away from home for the first time is going to do when he walks onto a college campus is to survey the social scene and see how he can best fit in. He will quickly find that the easiest way to do so is to party.

Certainly no student who sits down and pores over the medical records would come to the conclusion that getting drunk is good for him. He does know, however, that it will get him accepted by his peers. Because of this, it seems obvious to me that if the peer pressure were different the behavior would also be different. What if, as each new crop of college freshmen walked on campus, they perceived that 95% of their fellow students thought that getting drunk was low life behavior? Would they be as eager to get drunk and brag about it to their friends as they are now? I don't think so.

This is not solely confined to drunkenness either. It seems to me that there is great conformity of thought in the moral and spiritual realms on college campuses these days. Most of the students I speak to at Penn State will vehemently claim that they have come up with their moral and spiritual beliefs on their own, and that they would never sink so low as to get them by conforming to a religion or holy book. The problem is, the vast majority of them think a like. I believe you will find that the same thing is true on your campus. This is either an amazing coincidence, or they are conforming without realizing it.

For instance, if you ask the average student on campus what he thinks about drunkenness, sexual promiscuity, abortion, and homosexuality, you will get the same pro-choice answer from almost anyone. They will tell you that they may or may not approve of the behavior themselves, but they don't believe that they have the right to tell others how they should live. Universities promote this as the intellectual and enlightened way of thinking. By contrast, those who take a stand against these behaviors are considered to be narrow-minded and backwards. This is used at universities today to control thought in much the same way, as do the homosexual activists that I mentioned in a previous e-mail. I believe this is what is causing many of the students to conform.

In other words, if you agree with the above mentioned morals and believe that all religions are equally right, then you are a kind, open minded, generous, and thoughtful person, but if you do not, then you are a mean-spirited, narrow-minded bigot. Because of this intense peer pressure, most students will at least outwardly consent to this way of thinking—with many embracing it wholeheartedly. The question is whether this pro-choice attitude is really one of enlightened intellectualism or just plain ignorance. If you hadn't already guessed, my view is that it is one of ignorance.

The way I usually try and show this to skeptical students—and you may want to try this also—is to ask them what they think about something as obviously immoral as murder. Virtually every time they will tell me that they think it is wrong. There is absolutely no pro-choice sentiment in them at all. Do you see that when they know something is wrong, they are not pro-choice? It's when they are ignorant that they resort to it.

I do not really blame the students for this ignorance. It is simply how they have been educated to think. The reason for this is that our primary way of understanding the world around us has come from the philosophy of the Enlightenment. This philosophy claimed that we could only know that which we could apprehend through our reasoning. God was left out, and man became the measure of all things.

The flaw in this philosophy soon became evident, as man, when left to him, not only failed to come to an agreement as to what was right and wrong, but also often changed those morals that he had previously agreed upon. We can see this in our own society, as less than fifty years ago we believed abortion to be wrong, and now it's legal in all fifty states. In the 1950s few would have even considered the possibility of homosexuality being right, and now many are accepting of it. For most of our country's history we believed Christianity to be the only true religion. Now a sizable number believe it to be only one of many which are equally true. Who knows what we will believe in another fifty years. Because of this, many have given up ever knowing what is the truth and have gone to the default position of being pro-choice. Ironically, the Enlightenment has not brought us to knowledge and understanding, but to ignorance and confusion.

Many bright young students will graduate college knowing many useful things, but they will be ignorant of why they exist and how they should live their lives, and worse yet, will have been given no tools with which to answer these extremely important questions. Is it any wonder that so many resort to drunkenness and lives of materialism and pleasure? The only way to right the problem is to allow God—and His ability to reveal Himself—back into our way of knowing the world around us. If it is possible to know who is the true God, then it is possible to know the right religion, and by extension the right morals. If not, then we are doomed to moral ignorance and spiritual bankruptcy.

Sometimes I wonder if parents know what awaits their sons or daughters as they send them off to college. Then again, maybe parents these days are fully aware and are in agreement with what the universities are teaching and what the students believe in. It is, after all, the philosophy most of them adopted during their college days in the '60s.

In any case, don't let the Devil get you down. These things are to be expected when you begin to infringe on what he sees as his territory. Try to stand your ground with your roommate without destroying the relationship. Remember, you are evangelizing him also.

Always here for you,
Uncle Greg

14

GOD'S REVELATION

Dear Aaron,

It is good to hear that your roommate took what you had to say fairly well. From what you wrote he seems to be a nice guy who is just off the narrow path at the moment.

Your conversation with him was interesting and dovetails nicely with my last e-mail, as he is clearly thinking along the lines of the Enlightenment. This has him believing that everything must be proven either by the scientific method or by philosophical logic. As I said before, he is typical of most Americans in that, although we believe in God, we don't believe that He will reveal Himself to us. As a result, we don't believe we can know who is the real God, and we therefore conclude that the right religion—and by extension the right morals—cannot be known. So all that can be expected of us is to believe what we think is right and to do what we think is best. In other words, do and believe anything we wish.

This, in my opinion, is the unofficial national religion of America. The logic is sound, but it is dependent upon the belief that God cannot be known, which is an idea dependent upon the Enlightenment way of thinking. If the Enlightenment was right, then we are right, but if it was wrong, then we are wrong.

On the one hand, everyone must decide for himself what he thinks about Enlightenment philosophy. On the other hand, whatever we choose to believe, we should at least be consistent, and I don't believe that we have been. For example, as Americans we tend to believe in the existence of a loving God, and at the same time we believe that He is unwilling to make Himself known to us.

Now I understand that God's ways are not our ways, but I think we are pretty safe in saying that for both God and man love is primarily relational. If we love someone, we want to know him or her, and to have him know us. So why, if we believe that God loves us, do we also believe that he is unwilling to make Himself known to us? It not only doesn't make sense, but it also seems as if we are randomly stringing together beliefs to fit our lifestyle.

Another aspect of love is that it always desires the highest good of another. It certainly seems to me that it is in our highest good to know our Creator. It doesn't seem like an act of love to leave us floundering in this fallen world, with all its traps and pitfalls, not letting us know what it is all about, or how to navigate through it.

If you can get your roommate to understand this, then you can inform him that if he wants to know the truth, he can begin to ask God to open up his eyes. Certainly he would have nothing to lose and everything to gain. If God never reveals Himself, then he simply continues to be ignorant of the truth. If he does, then your roommate will gain the knowledge of God. As I said, he has everything to gain and nothing to lose. This, of course, would hold true for everyone—not just your roommate.

The one problem you may run into is that many people, despite objections to the contrary, really do not want to know God, especially if this means obeying Him. This is particularly true of college students, who for the first time in their lives are out from under their parents' authority and can finally decide for themselves how to live. The last thing many of them want is a God with commandments, telling them what to do. This makes them particularly susceptible to Enlightenment thinking. They already want to choose their own beliefs and morals, so it is easy for them to buy into the idea that God cannot be known. In addition, we have become so intoxicated with the power of choosing our own morals and beliefs that this has become more important to us than being right and knowing truth.

One way to show your roommate and your fellow students that their way of thinking is foolish is to ask them to imagine that they are on their deathbed, looking back on their lives. Then ask them whether, at that moment, it will be more important to them to have done and believed as they pleased, or to have done what is right, and believed what is true. I think the answer is obvious, and this is the reason why the great saints of the ages would tell their disciples to always keep death in front of their eyes. It is only if we know what is important in death that we will we know what is important in life. It may sound a bit morbid to the American mind, but it helps to keep things in perspective.

Don't lose heart with your roommate, and don't let him come between you and your evangelism. Sometimes people have to explore the depths of sin before they reach out to God. That's the way it was for me, and maybe it's the same for him. Keep up the good work.

Love,
Uncle Greg

15

EVIDENCE FOR THE RESURRECTION

Dear Aaron,

Wow that was quick! Just a short while ago we were discussing your roommate's unfortunate dive into hedonism, and now you're staying up half the night discussing religion. I understand he hasn't stopped his pleasure-loving ways, but at least you were able to plant some seeds. Hopefully, when he hits the inevitable dead end that all those who live for pleasure do, he'll remember some of what you said and turn to God.

I guess it doesn't surprise me that the conversation centered around the resurrection of Christ, since Christianity stands or falls on the veracity of that event. If Christ rose from the dead, then His claim of being the incarnate God must be taken seriously. If not, then we as Christians are the most foolish of all people, as we are worshipping a dead guy. That being said, there is no absolute proof of the resurrection, other than God's revelation to the human heart, but there is, in my opinion, some good circumstantial evidence.

To begin with, everyone is in agreement that a man named Jesus of Nazareth lived and died some 2,000 years ago, and that shortly after his death, his disciples began to preach that he had proven himself to be the Messiah by rising from the dead. They also claimed that after His resurrection and before He ascended into Heaven, He had spent a period of forty days teaching them all they would need to know to begin this new religion.

Now, I think your roommate would agree that this claim is either true, or the disciples lied. There doesn't appear to be any middle ground.

Maybe, if the disciples story was that after Jesus' death they were all depressed and sitting around the campfire when suddenly His face appeared in the flames smiling at them, as if to say everything was going to be all right so proceed with the mission, then we could all agree that it may have been a mass illusion stemming from their depressed state, and the shock they had just been through. When, on the contrary, the disciples claim that a risen Jesus taught them for forty days after the resurrection, then all ideas of a mass illusion must be set aside.

If your roommate will agree that the disciples were either telling the truth or lying, then the question to ask him would be, "If they were lying, what was their motivation?" The Jews at the time had a perfectly valid religion. Their problem was not a lack of religion but oppression by the Romans. Remember, the Jews during that period were looking for a messiah, but they were looking for a messiah to deliver them from Rome, and the disciples were preaching one who came to deliver them from sin and death. They weren't even preaching a messiah about which their own people wanted to hear! Consequently, many of the religious leaders began to persecute them. They were rejected by their own people, beaten, whipped, stoned, all but John martyred, and none of them ever recanted. Since they never tried, nor obtained, fame or fortune in their lifetimes, it escapes me as to what their motivation could have been to dedicate their lives and die for what they would have known to be a lie.

Ask your roommate, if under similar circumstances, either he or anyone he knows would have done the same. If not, then at least in my opinion, this is pretty powerful evidence that the disciples fully believed that Jesus had risen from the dead. In fact, if you read what they wrote and how they lived and died, it seems obvious that they believed this with all of their heart. What else other than the resurrection could have caused this belief? Once again, they were obviously not deceived, and it doesn't make sense that it was all just a charade. I'd be interested to hear your roommate's opinion.

While you are at it, ask him about Paul. Remind him that Paul was a rising star in the Jewish religion who called himself a Pharisee and a disciple of Gamaliel. He was so angered at this new sect of Judaism that was preaching what he considered to be a false messiah that he actually went to other countries to track down its adherents and to bring them back to Jerusalem for prosecution.

One day, seemingly out of the blue, he began to preach the very faith he had been persecuting. He claimed that as he was on his way to Damascus Syria, he was confronted by the risen Christ, he was blinded, and in essence he was asked why he was banging his head against the wall. He was then taken to Damascus, and after three days being prayed for by a believer, had his sight restored, was baptized, and then began preaching Jesus as the Christ. As a result of this, Paul lost his job and standing in the community, was beaten, whipped, stoned, imprisoned, and eventually martyred. He never sought or obtained fame or fortune nor did he ever recant in his lifetime.

On top of all of this, when Paul wrote his letter to the Corinthian Church and was speaking to them about the resurrection, he told them that upwards of 500 people had seen Jesus after he had risen, and most of them were still alive. Essentially, he was challenging them to contact these witnesses and was confident that they would back up his claim. Would Paul have gone out on such a limb if he were making it all up? That would have been unlikely at best.

The key to this whole puzzle is motivation. Obviously Paul was not deceived by a clever argument or bribed by poverty stricken disciples, to leave everything and die for a lie. There is no reason to believe that either Paul or the disciples were deceived. They knew whether or not Jesus had risen from the dead. Again, what your roommate has to come up with is a reasonable motive if it was all a lie. If he does come up with one, be sure to let me know, because in all of my years of evangelizing I have yet to hear any that make even a little sense.

All of these circumstances may not prove to your roommate that Jesus rose from the dead, but it should at least be enough to get him thinking and maybe seeking for answers. Keep up the good work, and I'll be praying for him and for you.

With much love,
Uncle Greg

16

HELL

D ear Aaron,

I can't say I was surprised to read your latest e-mail. Doctrinal disagreements have been a part of even the most laid back Protestantism from the beginning, and Hell can be a very controversial topic. I understand your distress that the conversation got rather heated, but hopefully there are no ill feelings, and you all parted friends. In the future do your best to put forth your ideas while remaining a peacemaker. I know this is a difficult role to play, but it is necessary in any Protestant fellowship. I must say it is encouraging to hear that discussions such as this are still going on in university dorm rooms, even if they are rare.

Your e-mail was a little hard to follow. I realize it was late, and you were still a bit confused by all that was said, but I think your intuition was sound if a bit hazy. I believe your friends are laboring under a common misunderstanding of Hell. This misunderstanding states that God gave us a law in order to judge us, and He is so offended when we break it that He needs to punish us in order to satisfy His justice. Fortunately, Jesus steps in and satisfies God's wrath for us. So, if we repent before we die, God will forgive us, but if we don't, His justice demands that He torment us forever in Hell. To put it another way, God has come to Earth in order to save us from Himself. As in many misunderstandings, this way of thinking contains just enough truth to be plausible, and just enough error to unnecessarily turn people off.

To begin with, God gives us a law in order not to judge us, but to help us. As I believe I mentioned in a previous e-mail, God knows that we are largely ignorant and imperfect, and if left on our own we tend toward selfishness and destruction. So, as a good Father, he gives us rules in order to help keep us from going astray. If God gets angry when we break these rules—and remember he does not have human emotions—it is because He knows what breaking them will do to us. God's anger is born out of love.

Some say—as your friends did the other night—that when we sin it is such an affront to God's holiness that He turns his back on us. In fact, the opposite is true. When we sin we turn our backs on God. He never leaves us: we leave Him. For example, God tells us not to get drunk because it is damaging to us. If we get drunk anyway, what we are saying to God is, "Thank you for looking out for me, but I'm on my own now, and I'm going to do what I want." Your roommate is a good example of this. God has not left him: he has left God.

Secondly, God has no need to satisfy his justice. In fact, God has no needs at all. If we say that God has a need, we make him less than divine. He then becomes subordinate to this need, which rules over Him, and which He is driven to satisfy. So then, I hear you ask, does God get jealous when we walk away from Him? Is that why he punishes us? No, once again, God is not subject to human emotions. When the scriptural writers give God such emotions, it is so we can understand Him in a human way. In His divine essence, God cannot be comprehended. There is no need or emotion in God according to which He is required to punish us. When we turn from Him we become sinful. If we carry this sinfulness into eternity, then the love of God, which was supposed to be paradise to us, becomes a torment instead.

I know this can be difficult to understand since we tend to see love only in its positive characteristics, such as forgiveness, mercy, and grace. We forget that it is love that condemns sin, and all sin is an offense against love. Whether it is against God, our neighbor, the creation, ourselves, or even our enemies, the transgression is always against love. It doesn't matter whether it is lust, greed, envy, fornication, or abortion; if we sin we have fallen short of perfect love.

Remember, Jesus came to enable us to love perfectly and live forever, loving and being loved by God and others. If we go into eternity sinful, the love of God will expose and condemn our sin, filling us with the torment of guilt, which like a worm, will eat away at us forever. Our minds will become darkened, and instead of running to God in repentance, we will see Him as our tormenter, and flee from Him forever. Just please bear in mind that it will be our sins, in the presence of the love of God, that will be doing the tormenting.

By the way, you will notice that in this understanding, Hell is not the absence of God. This is what the sinner ultimately wants, and so it would not really be Hell to him. It is the presence of God, from which it is impossible to get away, that the sinner hates, and it is this that ultimately becomes his judgment. According to this way of thinking, Hell is eternal not because God is unwilling to forgive, but because man is unwilling to repent. He may have some sort of remorse for his sin, but not the kind that leads to true repentance. Hell is not the fault of God but of man.

The reason many have rejected the idea of Hell is that, on the one hand, they were told that God is merciful, loving, kind, and forgiving, but on the other hand, He is so harsh that if you break even one law, and don't repent before you die, He will send you to Hell and keep you there forever. Since they didn't want to rid themselves of a loving God, the only way for many to reconcile this apparent contradiction is to rid themselves of Hell. After all, how can one love a God from whose wrath he is seeking to escape? If we see things in the way I've been trying to relate to you, there is no contradiction, because it is not God, but man, who is creating his own Hell, and keeping himself there forever. It is man who is condemning himself. Ultimately, of course, God must also reject him and cast him out, but only after man has fully condemned himself.

On the more positive side of things, when the Son of God, in the person of Jesus Christ, took human flesh, He perfected human nature by uniting it to Himself. Through His incarnation, life, death, resurrection, and ascension into Heaven, He defeated sin and death for us, and placed humanity, as represented by Himself, at the right hand of God. So, if we are baptized into, and commune with God through Jesus Christ, He will ultimately enable us to love perfectly. This is so that in eternity, the love of God will be paradise to us, as it was always meant to be. It is important that your friends understand that God has come not to save us from His wrath, but to save us from ourselves.

Some may ask about the Lake of Fire and whether this image is to be taken literally. If I understand the Fathers of the Church correctly, when the writers of the scriptures were speaking of earthly things they spoke literally, but when speaking of eternal things, they used earthly language to help us to understand that which we have never experienced. So, as I alluded to earlier, the fires of Hell likely indicate the fiery torment of our sinful passions burning within us. The darkness would be that which the mind and conscience are plunged into, and the worms eating at our soul would be the guilt and shame that gnaws at us because of our sin. This is why the Church is so intent at calling people out of their sins. It's not to be condemning, or holier than thou, but because we know something of the awful consequences of not doing so.

I hope this helps at least a little. I'm glad to hear that you and your friends are passionate about religion. It is good to see, and it warms an old man's heart. Well, maybe not such an old man, but I am warmed nonetheless. God Bless.

Encouraged and hopeful,
Uncle Greg

17

PROTESTANTISM

D ear Aaron,

I rather suspected this would be next on the list. I guess I even set it up by some of the remarks in my last e-mail. Before we get to it though, I must say I am glad that some of what I had to say about Hell made sense, and I am thrilled that you are all still friends. I've seen way too many friendships break up over doctrinal differences.

As far as Protestantism is concerned, I wasn't sure if you knew that I had converted to Eastern Orthodoxy a few years back, and apparently you did not. Before I get into the reasons why I converted, let me first of all be clear as to what I am not saying. I am not saying that Protestants are going to Hell or are not Christian. So please don't take what I am about to say in that way.

There were two basic reasons why I left Protestantism. First, through much studying of the Church Fathers and the history of the Church, I came to believe that Orthodoxy was the true expression of Christianity. Secondly, the two pillars of Protestant Christianity collapsed before my eyes. When they fell, all of Protestantism fell with them. To be more specific, I came to believe that *sola scriptura*, or "the Bible alone," and *sola fida*, or "faith alone", were neither biblical nor did they work in real life. As I am sure you know, the phrase "the Bible alone" means that the Bible is the sole authority of Christianity, and "faith alone" means that our salvation is accomplished without any works on our part.

This personal transformation of mine began when after months of debating an Orthodox student on campus, he finally challenged me to find the idea of the "Bible alone" in the scriptures. This occurred late on a Friday afternoon so I told him that I would check out my resources over the weekend and get back to him on Monday. I should have suspected the outcome when I didn't have the scriptures to such an important doctrine at my fingertips. Anyway, after an entire weekend of searching I came up empty. The best I could do was to find one passage that said that the scriptures were profitable towards certain ends, and another which said not to go beyond that which is written. The first one did not say that the scriptures were the only thing profitable towards those ends, and the second was specific to only one issue, and so could not be generalized to all of Christianity. In any case, neither one was making the claim that the scriptures were the sole authority.

At the same time, I did a word search on tradition, hoping to show my friend that the scriptures put it in an unfavorable light. What I discovered was that when Jesus spoke of the tradition of the Pharisees, He had nothing good to say, but when St. Paul spoke of the apostolic tradition, he had nothing bad to say. Imagine my chagrin, as a die hard Protestant, when I discovered that not only did the scriptures fail to express *sola scriptura*, but that on the contrary they exalted tradition. Then to make matters worse my friend showed me a scripture that said that the Church was the pillar and ground of truth. In other words, the Church was the foundation and upholder of the truth. By this time I was reeling. If the Church and her tradition was the authority, then the obvious question from the Protestant point of view was, "Which church?"

You see, Aaron, what I slowly came to realize was that since the Bible has no ability to actually speak, in a concrete as opposed to a figurative sense, then it's up to the individual reading it to decide for himself what he thinks it means. He may check with other sources, but in the end, and this is the ultimate outcome of *sola scriptura*, he is his own authority. Since we all tend to read the scriptures differently, we naturally split up into different sects and denominations. With so many to choose from, which church could possibly be the pillar and ground of truth?

This is when I began to realize that the doctrine of *sola scriptura* did not work in real life. I had always known that the splits and divisions in

Christianity were not right, but now I was seeing that what created all those divisions was one of Protestantism's foundational beliefs. Everything seemed to be turning upside down. The conclusion I finally came to was that since Christianity is a revelation given to the apostles by God through Jesus Christ, then if there was a true church, it had to be one that was there in the beginning with Christ and is still here today, without changing the doctrine or manner of worship. As I said earlier, after much research I came to believe that Orthodoxy is that Church, but we can talk about this at another time if you are interested.

The second pillar of Protestant Christianity that collapsed in front of me was the idea of justification by faith alone. Whereas the scriptures make it clear that we are saved by grace through faith, they do not say we are saved solely by faith. In fact, St. James says in his epistle, "You see now how that by works a man is justified and not by faith only." This doesn't mean that we make ourselves good enough for God, but that salvation is the process of taking a sinful, mortal, human being, and making him Christ-like and eternal. Our works, then, have a part in this process.

Too often in Protestantism, salvation is reduced to a one time only repentance of sin and faith in Jesus. The process of becoming Christ-like, when theology books mention it at all, is presented as an addition to, and not a part of salvation. This is how Protestants can believe in justification by faith alone. On the one hand, if all of salvation is accomplished when one first believes, then there is no place for works. On the other hand, if salvation is the process of becoming Christ like, then prayer, fasting, keeping the commandments, going to church, and so on, all become part of one's salvation. I came to believe that this was more scriptural, historical, and works better in real life than does the once and done Protestant idea.

For instance, Paul says that our salvation is nearer now than when we first believed, and Jesus says that he who endures to the end will be saved, both of which indicate some sort of process. But also, if all of our salvation was accomplished the moment we first believed, then what is the purpose of the rest of Christianity? Why does Jesus give us all these commandments, doctrines, and practices? I guess for some they may become a way of judging or maintaining their salvation, but they are never a part of salvation itself.

The very reason why many Protestants are so comfortable with all of the differences in their doctrines and beliefs is that they don't see how they apply to their salvation. Why does it matter what one believes about communion, baptism, confession, free will, and so on, if we've already been saved and made ready for Heaven? They only matter if salvation is an on going process.

Finally, I think what you'll find, if you pay close attention when you are reading the scriptures, is that most, if not all of the time, when they speak of grace and faith, works will follow close behind. This is because, as St. James says, "Even so faith, if it hath not works, is dead, being alone." They were meant to fit together as a seamless whole and not to be ripped artificially apart.

Well, there you have it. At least in part this is why I am no longer Protestant. Again, please don't take this as a condemnation of everything you believe. Obviously we have a lot in common. Just take it as a friendly challenge to look a little deeper and to see if these things are true. As Christians we should always be seeking after truth and never think that we have arrived and know it all.

With much trepidation,
Uncle Greg

18

ROMAN CATHOLICISM

Dear Aaron,

Once again, no, I am not saying that you will go to Hell if you are not Orthodox. Although it is typical in Protestant thinking to boil everything down to Heaven and Hell, it is not so in Orthodoxy. I am simply saying that since Orthodoxy is the true expression of Christianity, then that is where your salvation will be best accomplished.

I certainly did not mean to upset you by what I wrote. I would just hope that you would keep an open mind, and be willing to look into it. It seems to me that, in general, Protestants can be very open-minded when it comes to other denominations. Conversely, when it comes to Orthodoxy and Roman Catholicism, their minds immediately shut down, and they won't even look into the claims that are being made. I guess I was like that when I was Protestant so I'm not condemning you, and I do realize that the claim that we make is a pretty intimidating one. I would only ask that you don't shut yourself off to it without first checking it out.

The answer to your inquiry about Roman Catholicism is that, yes, I did look into it, and no, I did not reject it because of the Crusades and Inquisitions. As I mentioned last time, after the pillars of Protestantism collapsed before my eyes, I began to inquire as to whether there was a church which began with the disciples—and is still here today— which has not changed its doctrine or manner of worship. These criteria narrowed my search down to Orthodoxy and Roman Catholicism. My assumption from the beginning was that any organization that had been around for 2,000 years would have had its share of evil deeds and doers in its past. So I wasn't concerned with such things as Crusades and Inquisitions.

The place where I began my search was with the infallibility of the Roman Catholic Pope. Because of the discussions I had engaged in with the Orthodox student I mentioned in my last e-mail—and at the same time with a Roman Catholic grad student—I knew that there were differences between the two Churches. It seemed reasonable to me, that, if because of an anointing of infallibility, the Pope could not err when he made pronouncements on faith and morals, then when it came to the differences between the two Churches, the Latin Church would have to be right. On the other hand, if there was no evidence that the Early Church believed in papal infallibility, then that would be an indication that Rome had added to the faith, which would disqualify it from being the true and complete Church.

In addition, it seemed to me that this would have been a very important doctrine and therefore should have been written about extensively by the Fathers. I already knew that the Apostles hadn't written about it. This was disconcerting considering how important this understanding would have been for the administering of the faith. The one scripture that the Roman Catholic Church pointed to in Matthew 16, about Peter being the rock upon which the Church was built, was hardly a treatise on infallibility.

To make a long story short, I began to search the Church Fathers for evidence that they believed in this infallible anointing. What I found was that over the period of time that the Eastern and Western Churches were together as one, which was approximately 1,000 years, the Fathers wrote over and over again about every conceivable Church doctrine, but even with the best Roman Catholic sources I possessed, I could not find one reference to infallibility. I couldn't even find a Church Father who wrote against it, which would have at least let me know that someone had written for it. I concluded from this overwhelming silence that in whatever light the Church saw Rome, it didn't see her bishop as infallible.

This became exceedingly clear when I first heard—and then read for myself—that the Third Council of Constantinople in the year 681 condemned and anathematized a pope of Rome by the name of Honorius. This is one of the first seven councils of the Church and is agreed upon as being authoritative by both Rome and the Orthodox. To anathematize someone means to condemn and eliminate the said person from the Church. It made no sense to me at the time, and it still doesn't, that an infallible bishop could be anathematized for heresy. My conclusion was that infallibility was an addition to the faith, and I therefore ruled out Roman Catholicism as being the true church.

At the same time I looked into one other issue, and that was the debate over the *filioque*. The *filioque* was an addition to the Nicene Creed, "the" creed of Christianity, which along with the Western claim of papal authority ultimately split the Church. In agreement with John 15:26, the Creed that was agreed upon during the first two councils of the Church read in part, "and I believe in the Holy Spirit who proceeds from the Father." The Roman Catholic Church sought to unilaterally change this statement to read, "…the Holy Spirit who proceeds from the Father and the Son." *Filioque* translates from the Latin to *"and the Son."*

This change made no sense either biblically, as shown by the scripture in John 15, or in the Church's understanding of the Trinity. As you know, our understanding of the Trinity is that God is three persons and yet is still one God. In light of this, every characteristic ascribed to the Trinity must either be shared by the three—indicating one God—or specific to the one—showing separate persons. When the Roman Church claimed that the Holy Spirit proceeds from the Father and the Son, she gave a characteristic (bringing forth the Spirit) to two members of the Trinity. This was never done before, nor has it ever been done since. Again this made no sense given our understanding of the Trinity.

Another problem with the *filioque* has to do with where we place the unity of the Trinity. The West, through Augustine, said that this unity was in the common essence shared by the three persons. The East answered that the unity was in the person of the Father. If the West is right, then the Holy Spirit can proceed from the Father and the Son by way of the common essence. If the East is right, then the Holy Spirit can only proceed from the Father, as the Son can only be begotten of the Father.

The problem for the Catholic Church is that the Creed, beginning with the statement "I believe in one God the Father almighty," puts the unity of the Trinity in the person of the Father. The only way the Western understanding could work is if the Creed stated, "I believe in one God the common essence almighty," which it clearly does not. If it did, it would remove the personhood of God. So for me at least the insertion of the *filioque* seemed to be a clear doctrinal error.

As I continued to look into it I discovered other differences between the two Churches, but these initial ones were enough to convince me that Rome had strayed from the faith. To this day I can find no such doctrinal changes in the Eastern Church, and that is why I am now Orthodox and not Roman Catholic.

In conclusion, it seems to me that whereas Protestant churches tend to subtract from the faith, the Roman Catholic Church tends to add to it. What they have in common is a propensity, beginning with human logic, to change the Faith as they deem necessary. This makes them both man-centered institutions, and so they tend to be seen by many in the Orthodox Church as two sides of the same coin.

I know this has been a lot to spring on you all at once. I only hope that whatever decision you end up making will be done after a thorough investigation of the facts and not be an emotional reaction one way or the other.

With much love,
Uncle Greg

19

EVANGELICALISM

Dear Aaron,

It doesn't sound as if you quite made it to the last line of my previous e-mail. I'm not sure that staying in your church because you enjoy it and because your friends are there qualifies as a thorough investigation of the facts. Not only do I disagree with your assertion that all churches are essentially the same, although I understand how one who is Protestant could hold that position, but I also think that a great deal of Protestantism has done away with most of the reasons to go to church at all.

The vast majority of Protestants, and I guess I'm talking primarily of Evangelicals, do not believe that baptism is necessary for salvation, that confession made to a priest is effectual for the forgiveness of sins, or that communion is the body and blood of Christ. In other words, they have done away with the sacraments, and in doing so have removed most of the reasons for going to church.

These days you don't even have to go to church to worship or to hear a sermon preached. All you have to do is put on a worship tape and listen to your favorite preacher on T.V. If the truth were known, the only reason most Evangelicals go to church at all is to spend time with other believers, and this is only because of their fear of being led astray due to lack of fellowship. One could accomplish the same thing by tuning into a respectable Sunday morning televangelist, and having some good Christian friends. It should come as no surprise, therefore, that many churches have found the need to be more and more entertaining to entice people to come in.

This is the primary reason why most evangelical worship has turned into more of a multimedia rock concert than anything the Apostles would have recognized. I believe this came about when as many churches began to see their membership declining, they resorted to the time-honored Protestant tradition of looking to the culture to see what the people wanted and then giving it to them. They eventually came to the conclusion that what most people want today is fun and good times. So they took the rock music, to which everybody loves to party, and brought it into the church. Now they could offer the faithful Heaven, and along with it, a great time getting there. As I heard one person exclaim after a particularly raucous worship service, "The church throws the best parties!"

Many would ask why it matters if you lure people in with party music, if after you get them there, they can be preached to and possibly converted. The problem here is not with the initial profession of faith, which can happen anywhere, but with what happens afterwards. The fact is that most people obtain their understanding of the faith more through worship than through listening to a sermon. Unfortunately most don't remember a sermon ten minutes after they leave church. The worship on the other hand gets into their heart and stays with them.

Since today's Evangelical worship is focused more and more on an emotional experience, what you find is people leaving a service conversing about whether or not they have felt God. Now tell me, Aaron, what does God feel like, or just what is the God emotion? I think what Evangelicals are feeling are emotions stirred by the music, and they are mistaking these sensations for the experience of God. Not only were all the great saints of the ages distrustful of emotions, since they can change so rapidly, but also you'll find nowhere in the scriptures where the writers speak of "feeling God." They write about knowing God, having visions of God, understanding God, even becoming like God, but never feeling God.

One problem with all of this is that when tragedies happen in life, and these feelings of God can no longer be produced, then those who have bought into this system begin to wonder why God is no longer with them. I believe this is why so many Christian bookstores are stocked with books trying to assure the faithful that God is still with them when it hurts. Many Evangelical Christians have become so tied to their feelings that when they can no longer stir up the "God emotion," they think He has abandoned them.

Another problem, along these same lines, is that since these services are designed to be fun and exciting, many believers begin to think that life as a Christian should be equally fun and exciting. As a result, not only are many churches teaching that our lives as Christians should be filled with health, wealth, and prosperity, but virtually none are teaching the true Christian message of picking up our cross and denying ourselves. It is very important to understand that we will act as we worship. If our worship is a party, we will see the Christian life as a party. If our worship is ascetical, we will see the Christian life as ascetical. You can decide for yourself in which direction the Evangelical world has gone.

In addition to all of this, rock music is not conducive to communicating theological concepts. It is more inclined towards relatively simple, emotional verses about loving Jesus. Now there is certainly nothing wrong with loving Jesus, but if all you've obtained from years of worshipping is an emotional attachment to Christ, then you haven't received very much. Don't get me wrong; I am not saying that worship should be boring and lifeless. I think that was the problem with the more mainstream Protestant denominations that led to the Evangelical rock and roll reaction.

I believe that Orthodox worship is the ideal, as it is both beautiful and God centered, with much of the faith being communicated weekly. In addition, it is done in a manner that allows the faithful to bring any emotion they have into it. If they are happy they can rejoice, if they are sad they can mourn. Since God is not tied to a feeling, he is understood to always be present, our emotional state notwithstanding.

Maybe an example will illustrate what I have been trying to say. A few years ago, I was talking to a student who told me that as a teenager he became interested in Christianity and began to attend a rock and roll church. At about the same time, his life outside of church began to fall apart. I don't remember the exact details, but it was along the lines of finding out that his girlfriend was on drugs, and his parents were getting a divorce. He said that he couldn't reconcile the happy, carefree persona he was expected to have in church with his life outside of it. He decided that something had to give, and since he couldn't get rid of his life, it was Christianity that had to go.

I hope this helps you to see that it does matter which church you attend. Both doctrine and worship are important and very much affect the life of the believer. Once again, I would greatly hope that you would take some time and look into this a little deeper. I know that between studies and social activities your time is limited, but if at all possible at least try and do some readings in these areas. My prayer is that we would all seek diligently for the truth and not merely be content with what is easy and convenient.

With much concern,
Uncle Greg

20

LOSS OF SPIRITUALITY

Dear Aaron,

I must say I am heartened to hear that your previous comments were made out of tiredness and frustration and were not necessarily your true feelings. As I said before, I know how it can be when your most cherished beliefs are challenged, especially when you have papers due and exams to take. Your frustration and bewilderment at some of the things I have been saying are also understandable. I must commend you, though, for your willingness to come back for more. It shows a certain desire to seek after truth, and that is indeed a rare commodity these days. There are many in these spiritually confusing times that would have given up thinking about these things all together.

At any rate, your difficulty in seeing the connection between doctrine and spirituality is certainly understandable, and your assertion that your church is very spiritual despite its doctrine is also understandable. Most people today see doctrine as the domain of the theologians, and spirituality as dealing largely with how one feels, or what one experiences in church or prayer. Therefore many have come to see doctrine as almost irrelevant, as long as they can continue to have certain experiences during their services. I suspect this may be the case with you.

In my opinion, Jesus showed this separation between doctrine and spirituality to be an artificial one when he said that those who worship him must do so in Spirit and in truth. He went on to say that his Spirit is the Spirit of Truth, and that it is the truth that will set us free. I think one can deduce from this that Jesus does not separate his Spirit—and by extension our spirituality—from the truth. We must have one to have the other.

One of the reasons why most Protestants have difficulty seeing this is that they have a faulty view of salvation. This has led them to a false unity that is based more on a cosmic judicial system than on doctrine. As I mentioned in an earlier e-mail, most Protestants believe that salvation consists solely in God declaring them to be "not guilty" once they have believed in Jesus and repented of their sins. After this pronouncement they are expected to do two things. The first is to believe in a few of what they call core doctrines, such as the incarnation, the virgin birth, and the death and resurrection of Christ. This shows that they have become Christian. The second is to keep certain morals, such as sexual purity, and sobriety, to show that their life has been changed.

Starting from this rather juridical viewpoint, most of the doctrines of Christianity become unnecessary for one's salvation. This is where we get the very Protestant idea of primary and secondary doctrines. They unify around the "primary" doctrines and agree to disagree on the "secondary" ones. Not only does this viewpoint have no standing in the scriptures, but I also think one might want to question the Protestant understanding of Christianity if that understanding makes most of its doctrines irrelevant to salvation.

Once again, the process of becoming Christ-like is the Orthodox view of salvation. This is a lifelong process, and God has decided to work with us to bring it about. Because of this, any false understandings of the faith that we may have will hinder our progress. Since we must worship God in Spirit and in truth, and since it is the truth that sets us free, then all the doctrines of Christianity become important to our salvation. It is becoming Christ-like, and by extension drawing closer to God, which we consider to be true spirituality. It is the Devil who introduces lies and deceptions into the faith, and the Spirit of Truth cannot work with the spirit of falsehood.

Another thing that hurts our spirituality in Christianity today is the lack of asceticism, and specifically fasting. Once again, the goal of our salvation is to become Christ-like, and the Fathers of the Church have told us that one very important way to get there is through asceticism. To help us toward that end the Church has instituted regular times of fasting. Needless to say, most Protestant churches have done away with these all together. My focus here, though, will be on the Roman Catholic Church, who at one time followed many of these prescriptions, but has now left most of them behind.

Traditionally the Church has fasted from all meat, fish, and dairy products for forty days before Christmas. This is virtually unknown in Roman Catholicism today. The Lenten fast, which is also forty days of no meat, fish, and dairy, has declined into not eating meat on Fridays. This is hardly an ascetical labor. Traditionally, the faithful have fasted all food and drink from midnight, the night before a liturgy, until after communion the next day. All that is expected these days in the Catholic Church is to fast one hour before receiving communion. One can get up a little early, have a big breakfast, and still have plenty of time to fulfill that requirement. Many older Roman Catholics can still remember the weekly Wednesday and Friday fasts. This eventually was reduced to Friday only, and now is largely ignored all together.

On a slightly different note, but still on the topic of asceticism, the Church has traditionally stood during her services. Now, most Roman Catholic Churches have pews, so they can take a load off during the Mass. One does not even have to arise early Sunday morning to go to church any more as that requirement can now be fulfilled Saturday evening.

Are you beginning to see the lack of spirituality? Being spiritual is not an emotion, or how you feel during a service, but it is making progress in becoming like Christ and drawing closer to God. It is no wonder that most Protestant churches have lost this idea altogether, and many Catholic parishes are doing likewise. Truth, asceticism, and Christ likeness are inseparably bound together. If you lose one, you will to one degree or another begin to lose the others. Truth has been compromised. Asceticism and Christ likeness have been all but lost. If that is not a decline in spirituality then I am at a loss to know what is.

I hope these last few correspondences have helped you to see that correct doctrine, worship, and practices are essential to our salvation. It is a little bit sad that we even have to talk about these things as at one time they would have been considered to be self-evident. Again, please don't take that as a condemnation of you. It is just a symptom of the times in which we live. Who would have thought that spirituality would have come to be associated with an emotion elicited by pop music. The Devil must be dancing with glee.

Anyway, on a more upbeat note, I must say congratulations, and keep up the good work in school. It is exciting to hear that you are doing well, but then I always knew you would. After all you come from good stock!

Proud as always,
Uncle Greg

21

RELIGION IN SOCIETY

D ear Aaron,

I can surely appreciate your desire to take some time and think about our recent discussions. It certainly is a lot to take in all at once, and you need time to think it through and digest it. Maybe the upcoming break will help you to do so. I can also fully appreciate your frustration in not being able to get into very many good theological discussions on campus. In the midst of such an intellectual environment, you shouldn't have to be writing to your old uncle to talk theology.

I think part of the reason for this theological dearth you are experiencing is that, since religion is not important in our society, most people are not very well educated in it. It is the big black hole in most people's education, and amongst other things, it hurts our ability to understand the world around us. For instance, you cannot really understand a nation without first understanding its religion. It is hard for us to understand countries that are typified by religious fundamentalism when we see all religions as equally right. I must admit that our belief in this area baffles me, especially in light of the Christianity that has been the faith of the majority of our population for most of our history.

As you are well aware, Christianity declares Jesus to be God, and every other world religion says that he is not. Jesus is an actual person who walked the earth 2,000 years ago. So when we claim him to be God, we are not simply putting another name on the Great Spirit. We are, on the contrary, pointing to a specific person in history, and declaring Him to be the incarnate God. Now I think everyone can agree that He either is or He is not. If He is, then Christianity would be right about who God is, and all the other religions would be wrong. If He is not, then as Christians we are the most foolish of all people, as we would be worshipping a dead guy. This is why we have no choice but to say that Christianity is the only true religion, even if the prevailing wisdom in America today, is to declare all religions to be equally right.

By the way, this is another reason why there is not more value put on religion nowadays. Not only are we severely undereducated in this area, but also as soon as society makes the claim that all religions are equally right, it makes them all equally meaningless. Why seek out the truth if everything is true? To look at it from a slightly different angle, what value would there be in going to college, if no matter what you did while you were there, everyone was assured of graduating with an A average? How could you distinguish yourself, or make yourself look good to an employer? Sure, there would be a few self-motivated individuals who would go simply from a desire to obtain knowledge, but most would not bother.

This is the state of religion today. There are some self-motivated souls who do not buy into the prevailing wisdom and are seeking to find the true religion, but most don't bother. If all beliefs are equal, what is the point? Simply believe in God and be a nice person, and all will be fine. That's exactly what most people are doing. This is why it is hard to get into a good theological debate today even on a college campus. We've educated people not to care.

I guess this illustrates the need for more young men and women such as yourself to zealously evangelize. If the state is educating people to go to Hell, then we need to be educating them to go to Heaven. It may seem like an overwhelming task, but as long as God is with us, it doesn't matter who is against us.

You mentioned that it's getting close to finals, and you may not have time to write before the end of the semester. So I'd just like to say that it's been a pleasure corresponding with you. Hopefully I will see you over the Christmas holiday, and with your permission we'll pick up where we left off next semester.

With much love,
Uncle Greg

45835625R00057

Made in the USA
Middletown, DE
20 May 2019